# ARTS & CRAFTS HOUSES

Schiffer Publishing Ltd

4880 Lower Valley Road Atglen, Pennsylvania 19310

STEVEN PAUL WHITSITT
AND TINA SKINNER

Other Schiffer Books By The Author:

*Esherick, Maloof, and Nakashima: Homes of the Master Wood Artisans,*
    978-0-7643-3202-9, $49.99

*Handmade Houses,*
    978-0-7643-3203-6, $29.99

Other Schiffer Books on Related Subjects:

*Shingle Style Architecture for the 21st Century,*
    978-0-7643-3551-8, $49.99

*Palm Springs Mid-century Modern,*
    978-0-7643-3461-0, $29.99


Schiffer Books are available at special discounts for bulk purchases
for sales promotions or premiums. Special editions, including personalized
covers, corporate imprints, and excerpts can be created in large quantities
for special needs. For more information contact the publisher:

Schiffer Publishing Ltd.
4880 Lower Valley Road
Atglen, PA 19310
Phone: (610) 593-1777; Fax: (610) 593-2002
E-mail: Info@schifferbooks.com

For the largest selection of fine reference books on this and related
subjects, please visit our web site at www.schifferbooks.com
We are always looking for people to write books on new and
related subjects. If you have an idea for a book please contact us at the
above address.

This book may be purchased from the publisher. Include $5.00
for shipping. Please try your bookstore first. You may write for a free
catalog.

In Europe, Schiffer books are distributed by
Bushwood Books
6 Marksbury Ave.
Kew Gardens
Surrey TW9 4JF England
Phone: 44 (0) 20 8392 8585; Fax: 44 (0) 20 8392 9876
E-mail: info@bushwoodbooks.co.uk
Website: www.bushwoodbooks.co.uk

Photography Copyright © 2010 by Steven Paul Whitsitt

Text Copyright © 2010 Schiffer Publishing, Ltd.

Library of Congress Control Number: 2010939686

Designed by Stephanie Daugherty
Type set in Rennie Mackintosh ITCStd/Geometr231 BT

ISBN: 978-0-7643-3670-6
Printed in the United States

# CONTENTS

# DEDICATION

I dedicate this book to my father, Paul Whitsitt. I was shooting the images for this book when my family learned that my father had cancer. His battle was short and brutal, and he lost only a few weeks later. I was lucky to be able to spend his last few weeks with him.

Since I am a visual person, many of the memories I have of dad run through my mind like videos. Dad was tall, In my mind's eye, I see him walking with me down the main aisle of the store where he worked, with me having to take three or four steps to keep up with his one. It was always comforting to be able to scan a crowd and quickly find him towering over everyone else.

I can see him in all of the things that we built together, our family home, and barn, and countless other construction projects. He modeled a level of perfectionism, attention to detail, and craftsmanship that I try to emulate in everything that I do. He taught all of us a work ethic that borders on obsessive. When people accuse my sisters and me (and they frequently do) of being workaholics, we just look at them and say, "Yeah, what's your point?" I think that what we share is the sense of joy in working hard and striving for perfection.

Dad had an interest in photography when I was a boy. He took a class at the local community college, and took me into the dark room. I remember the magic of watching the black and white image appear in the developer. No matter how many times I've seen it, that magic never goes away. Later on, after he retired, Dad bought his first Nikon, by this time, I was a burgeoning professional, and he allowed me to teach him a few things. Once after I had been working for several years he confessed something to me. "You know when you first told me that you wanted to be a photographer, I thought well, that's a fine hobby, but you'll never make a living. I have to say, I was wrong, in all these years, you've never once needed a bail out." Call the papers, I was impressed that he could admit that, and it was a nice way to let me know that he was proud of me.

As I watched him just before he left us, his body diminished and weakened, I thought of a quote by the writer George Bernard Shaw, "I want to be thoroughly used up when I die. For the harder I work the more I live. I rejoice in life for its own sake." I looked upon my father lying there and thought, "Yes, indeed he is used up, but he lived his life with a richness, a fullness that will continue to inspire me for my remaining days." May I too be so used up. I can barely comprehend all of the ways that I will miss him. But I trust that those will be well balanced with the realization of all of the different ways that his influence is a part of me.

Steven Paul Whitsitt

# ACKNOWLEDGEMENTS

The following homeowners graciously and wholeheartedly said, "Yes," opening their homes for inspection and photography. In fact, many others did so as well, but time, budget, and the limitation of book pages precluded us from including them and it is hoped that we'll soon get to visit them for another wonderful volume. For starters, and because this would not have begun without her, Maurine St. Gaudens gets our extreme gratitude. She got the stone rolling, and the avalanche followed. As a restoration professional and expert on California art, Maurine knows all the important collectors, and, as a resident of Pasadena, she sees the best homes every day, including that of her own son, Roger Kintz, and her best friend and life partner, Chuck Mauch. We authors count her as a dear friend, and in addition to the opportunity to tour incredible homes in California, visiting Maurine ranked at the top of the whole experience.

Additionally, Morris J. Sheppard, whose career has included replicating and expanding upon the craftsman themes pioneered by his peers generations earlier, made introductions and shared his magic. Because of him, the beachfront home of super songwriter Jerry Leiber and his significant other, author and fashion designer Tere Tereba, is included in our book, along with the homes of Sofie and James Howard, and Paul and Lisa Norling.

And then there was Adam Janeiro. What a Los Angeles treasure. Adam is a realtor whose living is made selling homes, but whose passion is spent saving them. His knowledge of the Arts & Crafts districts of the city, and his shared passion with his clients, are at the heart of this book. You'll enjoy his website: www.recenteringelpueblo.com

The other homeowners featured in our book won our hearts, as well. In no particular order, we wish to thank Rob Bruce, Gisa & David Nico, L.B. Nye, Heather McLarty and Troy Evans, Steve and Eileen Wallis, Hunter Rochs, Jennifer Giersbrook, Mia and Gabriel Marano, Paul Casebeer and Ildiko Laszlo, Ulrik "Jeff" Theer and Lisa Ellzey, and Bonnie Fisher. You are all amazing—living in beautiful homes, putting your own stamp on them creatively, and collectively doing the world a great service in preserving architecture, antiques, and an incredible aesthetic. We thank you for your generosity on behalf of the many readers who will enjoy this book for generations to come.

# INTRODUCTION

Much has been written about the movement around the turn of the 19th century to counter the increasing urbanization and mechanization of human life. You're probably already familiar with the story, since you were drawn to this book by its title. Just in case you aren't, a short synopsis follows and, should this spark a newfound interest, you'll find a lifetime's reading in books dedicated to the history of the Arts and Crafts movement, including its great architectural and design leaders, the minutia of its important artisans, and its many disciplines.

Sophisticates in the early 1900s embraced the idea of individually crafted objects over the mass produced objects pouring forth from huge factories and assembly lines. Potters, woodworkers, blacksmiths, and glass blowers were celebrated for their skills, and an earthy and sometimes exotic aesthetic was sought. Japanese influence was strong, as that culture also celebrated a link between human skill and nature. The home itself was modeled after the simple, open homes of India, and named for them: the bungalow.

Like any other movement, the Arts & Crafts aesthetic became widely copied, and as cookie-cutter tract homes sprung up along new suburban streets, many were fashioned and furnished in the vogue style of the time. The bungalow became commonplace across the American landscape, built following mass-produced mail-order house plans distributed by companies like Sears, Radford, and Aladdin.

These homes are often found in the densely populated neighborhoods surrounding a city core, the first ring of homes built as a small city grew early in the 20th century. As subsequent rings spread from that city core, and car ownership became commonplace, these inner neighborhoods became less desirable. The homes were sold down the economic chain to new immigrants or rented to those who couldn't afford to buy. As a result, their original aesthetic was often not valued, and in many cases not preserved. Their humble proportions often gave way to larger buildings that reflected the growing fortunes of the city.

As a result, the homes and neighborhoods that have survived intact present a treasure for today's growing population of re-urbanites, who are returning to reclaim the heritage of community. These bungalows, when repossessed by the appreciative, become the perfect gallery in which to display treasures hunted down on the antiques market (at no small price). So, once again, an elite group, presumably with you numbered amongst them, has come to value the work of artisans who labored in those early years to create the items of daily use and adornment. Thanks goes out to those early sophisticates who realized the value of handmade and, through their patronage, helped preserve time-honored skills from extinction.

Each of the sixteen homes we photographed has lessons to share about arts and crafts style. For the woodworker, there are all manner of built-in cabinets and window seats, and molding profiles that will inspire you. For the mason, tile, stone, and brick fireplaces, walls, and columns will get your juices flowing. Glass artists will love the photography detailing lighting and stained glass windows. And for collectors, the displays created by others will give you endless ideas for living with your own treasures.

# PART ONE:
# THE BIG PICTURE
## EXTERIORS

In countless books on home design, I've begun each with the exteriors and worked my way inside. This time I was going to be different, just because it seemed like sometimes things should be different. Yet in the end, I came back to my set-in-stone opinion that it is logical to begin at the curb, with the first impression a home has to offer. No matter what one finds within, the home's exterior defines it.

The idea of the Arts & Crafts bungalow was lifted late from nineteenth century India, where colonists and Indians alike found value in a simple, open-room plan that allowed a flow of air and traffic. Big shady porches were paramount, and almost invariably found on the front of any self-respecting Arts & Crafts bungalow. The gables also faced front and center, with linear banks of casement windows—practical for ventilation and charmingly honest in their open faced presentation to the world. The craftsman's work in creating the home was never neglected, either. Wood rafters and beams were exposed to celebrate the joinery, and the importance of the home's frame. Nature, too, got her due in shingle and wood sheathing left bare or with a clear finish, or with stucco siding both practical and earthy. In each home, the elements of earth and craftsmanship are paramount to the design and reflective of the builder's values.

The façade of this home is a wonderful example of bungalow style. The gabled roof faces the street, inset by two smaller dormers balanced above the open porch. Exposed roof beams were given added ornamentation in this case to emphasize their beauty, and decorative timbers above the dormers and the extended porch gable evoke the Tudor style popular in the same era. The home sports both stucco and shingle finishes, both popular finishes of the era.

This home, designed by architects Train & Williams and built in 1911, is
on the Department of the Interior's National Register of historic houses.

Tudor style is evident in the exposed timbers that punctuate the stucco finish. Brick forms the underbelly of the structure, the running bond pattern complementing the formal style of the home.

A historic photo shows this home in its infancy, prior to mature landscaping and color photography, revealing its true potential. The home is characterized by its broad expanse and the unusual brick archway that opens under the front porch. The horizontal roofline extends prairie style to shelter this home, while stone columns and walls swoop and flare like a bungalow.

Projecting roof rafters celebrate the structure.

Matching sets of casement windows grouped in horizontal
bands and a low, flat roofline evoke classic prairie style.
This is further evidenced with a wood and stucco finish.

Projecting rooflines extend the eaves, emulating the prairie style sensibilities that co-evolved with the rise of arts and crafts design.

A sheltered porch is little used in the modern neighborhood, so only a small allowance was left for this classic Arts & Crafts characteristic on a shingle façade that maximizes interior square footage.

OPPOSITE:
Leaded windows follow the lines of a split level.

Wood shingles stained dark and heavy wood trim painted a contrasting wheat accentuate the features of a classic bungalow home. A broad entry and deep-set, shady front porch add to the inviting nature of these homes.

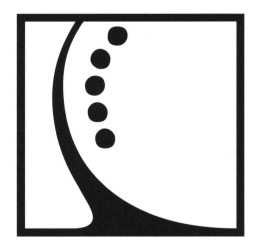

Extended rafters add definition to the dark face of a broad, gable face, typical of the California bungalow.

Swiss influence on this craftsman creates a somewhat different façade for this bungalow. The gabled ends of the first story face away from the street, while a dormer provides its fanciful, rounded face as a predominate feature. Stonework below creates a fortresslike surround for the classic, sheltered front porch.

Running courses of brick defy straight lines as they meander around chunks of white river stone jutting from the skirt of this home. Above, green board and batten accented with brick-red molding completes the rustic appeal.

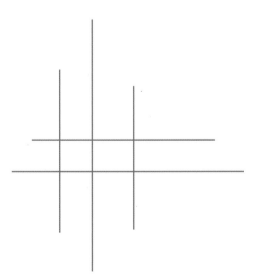

OPPOSITE:
Massive river stones ascend a rustic chimney, built solidly atop a flared base.

Rafters extend beyond the broad roofs and walls, and the base of the shingle walls flare—two characteristics definitive of bungalow style.

An impressive two-story façade presents the gable face and extended rafters expected in a craftsman home, along with the solid woodwork and shingle siding that characterize this school of architecture.

River stone and woodwork characterize this craftsman era home, with a peaked gable end that adds Tudor flavor to the mix.

This owner-built (ca. 1910) home presents the classic, modest gable front to passersby. Extended rafters and exposed beams celebrate the carpenter's skills.

The broad gable of a dormer presents the public face of this craftsman home.
Diamond panes in the upper window casements hint at the dwelling's Swiss influence.

The composer Carrie Jacob Bonds built this home near what is now the heart of Los Angeles, though it has been modified since the second floor was destroyed by fire. Shingle siding and stonework characterize this hill-top hideaway.

# Porches & Home Extensions

In our sentiments of neighborhood living dwells a dream of front porches, where neighbors drop by, tea is sipped, and news traded. The porch is sheltered from precipitation, breezy, and shaded when the weather is sweltering.

In fact, in earlier times these extensions of the indoors were important. Before central air conditioning, one did go out on the porch to cool off, and before television, this is where the evening entertainment was likely to take place. Today's citizens are more likely to retreat to hidden backyard spaces when they yearn to sit outdoors, and we can bemoan or celebrate as we see fit. Still, the front porches of these historic homes still serve as testament to days of yore, and style statements that grace the front of their home.

A shaded front porch is an expected amenity in a classic bungalow, extending the living space out of doors. A picture window is capped with leaded glass.

Wicker is a nice choice for furnishing the classic bungalow porch.

The owner plied a creative bent with eggplant and cool, leaf-green paint. The rich colors stand out against the stonework of a shady front porch.

**OPPOSITE:**
A backyard profile emphasizes a view into nature, and the home's colors tie it to the outdoors.

A privacy fence adds shade to one of the wide openings that characterize the bungalow porch.

A second floor terrace offers a view over the landscape in the back. Wood shingles act as a foil to handsome, two-toned wood trim.

Rustic furnishings are appropriate picks for a period porch.

An extensive arbor is under-hung with lighting and furnished with today's comfort-first furnishings featuring outdoor upholstery.

Trellis extends the living area, creating the sense of an outdoor room atop a raised patio. The four-post corner columns are extravagant reminders of the home's arts and crafts aesthetic.

A random mosaic of river stone and rough brick embody
the beauty of the handmade. Flared bases and projecting
rafters pay homage to the Arts and Crafts era.

## Stonework

The industrialist might like to see his bricks all perfectly aligned, running in perfect columns like disciplined soldiers, each precisely like the one to its left and right. The Arts & Crafts movement demanded the opposite. Imperfect bricks, and hard-to-define stones were valued individually, and spaces created to conform to their uniqueness.

The walls, chimneys, and columns photographed here are a testament not only to the mason's skill, but to his decision making and aesthetic. They evoke awe and embody the craftsman's love and respect for his medium.

OPPOSITE:
Brickwork is punctuated by the protrusion of clinkers, the melted and deformed bricks often discarded after removal from the kilns, but celebrated as little treasures by arts and crafts artisans.

A wall of smooth river stone and bricks is capped with canted brick.

Cast stone emulates wood, an aesthetic named *faux bois* by the French. This incredible fireplace graces a spacious entryway, complete with courtship benches where unmarried men might engage eligible women of the household in open-air conference. Enjoying the folly of their home's noteworthy feature, the homeowners have adorned a little alcove with a real bird's nest.

A river stone column contrasts with the relatively smooth finish of painted clapboard.

Extending the living space outdoors, river stone was carefully formed to create a fireplace and benches on the exterior wall of this arts and crafts home.

An archway of river stone creates a fortresslike entryway.

## LIVING ROOMS

In common bungalow homes, visitors enter into a foyer that connects via large open doorways to the living areas of the home. Then, as now, the living room was the public face of the family. These living areas are where proud homeowners are able to put on their best display of Arts and Crafts-era sensibility. In them are housed historic treasures, loved and lived with daily.

A coffered ceiling and the flat trim around windows and doorways form a framework for interior areas. Here antique furnishings and accessories are entirely in keeping with the home's original intent.

Stickley-style furnishings reflect the casual nature of this front sitting room, which opens to another sitting area beyond massive doorways flanking a central foyer. Careful restoration is revealing the original wallpaper. Beautiful, built-in bookcases with stained-glass grace either side of a big picture window on the far wall.

Framed by two stained glass windows, a massive, tiled fireplace surround forms a central focal point in this living room. The area has been lovingly furnished with period antiques with a taste for the exotic.

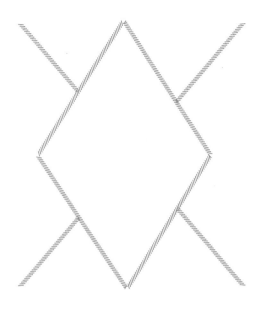

Cast concrete emulates stone in this chunky fireplace surround.

Flared wood columns supporting wooden beams bring
the architecture of the bungalow's exterior inside.

A cast stone fireplace introduces a rustic element to a room
encased in warm woodwork and furnished with period antiques.

Diamond panes in the windows indicate Swiss craftsman style. Wood paneling in
the room has been painted white in a more modern quest to brighten the space.

From an era that celebrated simplicity, nature, and the work of a craftsman, this is the perfect vignette. Stickley-style furnishings accompany a baby's rocking cradle, now filled with literature, and a basket of findings.

A barrel vaulted ceiling ends in arched murals on either side of this unique living area. A stone fireplace, original woodwork, and antique accessories lend historic context to furnishings that reflect a more modern pursuit of comfort.

BOTTOM ROW:
A fireplace takes center stage in a living room
outfitted with Stickley-style furnishings. Cast plaster
moldings add to the formality of the room.

Contemporary scale is accomplished with craftsman style for this built-in entertainment center by Morris J. Sheppard.

Mid-century furnishings merge with arts and crafts architecture beautifully in a living room anchored by a fireplace surround that celebrates the mason's skill.

OPPOSITE:
A corner fireplace of brick adorns half-paneled walls beneath a coffered ceiling.

A great room extending the depth of the house is put to work as both a sitting area and music room. Built-in cabinetry opens to this room as well as the kitchen, which is on the other side of the wall.

A cast stone fireplace warms a richly paneled room, also illuminated by two huge bay windows.

Crown molding takes on a distinctively arts and crafts appeal in the hands of woodworker Morris J. Sheppard.

Ceiling beams custom crafted by Morris J. Sheppard help create zones within an expansive room.

# DINING ROOMS

Built-in cabinets, buffet surfaces, paneled walls, and richly molded ceilings attest to the importance of the dining room in presenting a public face. For a homeowner who wants to recreate this aesthetic, this chapter is loaded with wonderful ideas for retrofitting a room with woodwork, glass, and lighting.

Built-in cabinetry, including a buffet counter, are original to the house, all carefully crafted to match the heavy molding around the generous windows.

Green walls are in keeping with the love of nature embodied in Arts and Crafts-era expressions. All of the furnishings are of the period, as are Oriental carpets that complement the beautiful wood flooring.

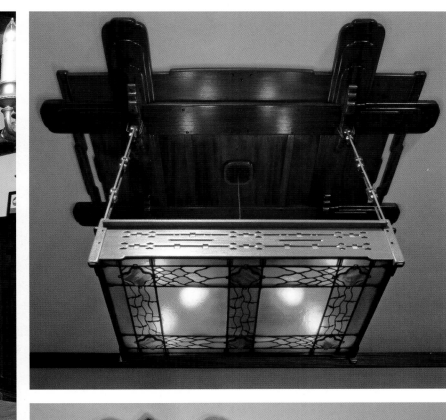

FAR LEFT COLUMN:
Antiques only in this dining room, a living history museum of dining in the Arts and Crafts era.

MIDDLE:
Leaded windows crown a built-in hutch, illuminated by original sconces.

Wood board and batting extends halfway up the walls of this dining area, in keeping with built-in storage and buffet space.

NEAR LEFT:
Crafted in beautiful cherry wood, screened half doors divide dining room from kitchen. The chandelier is a two-thirds scale reproduction of a lamp from Frank Lloyd Wright's Blacker House. The original fixture is now housed in the Los Angeles County Museum. For the reproduction, Morris J. Sheppard did the woodwork and John Hamm the glass.

A Craftsman-era frieze underlines woodwork on the ceiling and emphasizes the woodland tones.

Rich paneling, built-up layers of window molding, a plate rack, and crown molding give this room its architectural flare.

Curved glass china cabinets are an inherited treasure in this bungalow home. The glass is one notable luxury in a room literally surrounded in beautiful paneling and built-in storage space.

Irregular bricks create a rustic fireplace surround in a room richly paneled with wood. Above, exposed beams support a wonderful antique chandelier of stained glass and wrought iron. Built-in cabinetry fills a recess capped by diamond-paned windows.

Rich paneling and a built-in china cabinets distinguish this dining room. Leaded glass cabinet doors reveal chinaware, and in between an inset stained glass window serves as a centerpiece.

The beautiful grain patterns of quarter-sawn oak are showcased in a paneled dining room rich with built-in furnishings. Collected antiques preserve the room's original rich intent. An adjacent conservatory connects the room with a sense of outdoors, a convention treasured by the home's 1930s builders, and again by our generation.

## KITCHENS

Kitchens aren't what they used to be! These kitchens strike a balance between what was likely to be a spare room used primarily by servants or a relatively poor housewife, to a room that ranks on any fifty-cent house tour. In today's society, guests not only see the kitchen, they are likely to hang out here. If the room is big enough, most meals will be taken here, too.

An antique stove is the centerpiece in a spacious, serviceable eat-in kitchen.

An antique stove still serves household cooks.

A modern refrigerator is concealed behind wood panels sensitively designed to reflect arts and crafts styling. Antique lighting helps keep the authenticity of an updated kitchen, along with a collection of California paintings of the Arts and Crafts era.

Walnut pegs and butterflies punctuate a pine floor.

A wall cabinet is a testament to a woodworker's craft.

Colorful dinnerware is characteristic of the era.

An antique stove still works, though the owner isn't prone to a lot of cooking.

An antique icebox was our forefather's solution to refrigeration. This beauty has been retrofitted to refrigerate using electricity instead of ice blocks.

Original kitchen cabinetry was paired with a custom-made refrigerator and a retrofitted antique stove that are in keeping with past times. It is still impossible, however, to recreate the automatic dishwasher—previously a job done only by hand.

The palette of the sunny southwest finds its way into a kitchen trimmed in Mexican tile and adorned with cobalt paint.

Original woodwork preserves the arts and crafts nature of this expansive kitchen, modernized with appliances and marble countertops more suitable for contemporary food preparation.

Craftsman Morris J. Sheppard's period reproduction skills were employed to replace this kitchen's original plywood cabinetry with cherry.

## BEDROOMS, BATHS & BEYOND

Following is a sampling of other noteworthy Arts and Crafts-era legacies found
throughout the homes we photographed. Welcome to some of the more private
rooms, and thank you to those who allowed us access.

A fireplace warms a master suite. The lavish molding creates dual
mantels and pedestals so pretty they need no ornamentation.

A ball and claw-foot tub adds to the historic character of this bath, encircled by windows framed in classic woodwork. The chandelier and raised sinks are more contemporary in their sentiments.

An entry alcove serves as a music room furnished with antiques.

An antique cabinet is capped with marble that reflects the sensibility of early craftsman design, and plumbing reminiscent of the early days of water closets. The protruding frame of the medicine cabinet is a great example of the era.

An original toilet like this is a rare find in any historic home.

Walnut pegs and biscuits celebrate the workmanship in this built-in bathroom cabinet.

**NEAR RIGHT AND OPPOSITE:**
Flat, profile molding around windows
and the medicine cabinet lend a historic
architectural context to this spacious bath.

A pedestal sink is lit by antique lighting over a built-in cabinet and paneling of the era.

A pedestal sink sits like a sculpture under incandescent lights that dot the top beam of a cathedral ceiling.

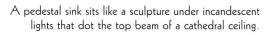

Lodgelike surrounds were the ideal in the Arts and Crafts era, and this attic escape literally creates a vacation getaway under the same roof. The leather furnishings and rustic accouterments are in keeping with the time period and the flared end-posts of the stairs mimic the flare given to posts on many facades.

Another living room emulates the rustic retreat aesthetic, with a bearskin rug front and center. The room is richly furnished with period antiques.

This sun room addition was built by the original owner in about 1911. Its slanted roof is a unique feature.

A foyer is characterized by dark woodwork that contrasts with the white walls.

# PART TWO: THE FINE DETAILS

## Doors

A massive oak door provides the visual impact necessary to stand out under the sheltered porch.

A leaded glass door evokes Wright sensibilities and embodies the tapered profile typical of bungalow exteriors.

Fanciful carved moldings frame the leaded glass window of this solid-wood front door.
Leaded glass sidelights classically framed in woodwork add further adornment.

Half sidelights flank a solid wood paneled door, fashioned three over two.

Diamond lights evoke Swiss style, set like lace around a heavy timber door.

A flared frame contrasts with the rich wood of a double front door,
featuring a screened front unusual in the California home.

Sidelights mirror the breadth of the front door, creating an incredibly expansive entrance that impresses from the outside and helps illuminate the interior.

Three beveled windows emphasize the massive nature of a front door, whose celebrated wood has withstood the test of time.

A solid oak door sits golden amidst shingles painted cocoa brown.

John Hamm crafted the glass for this massive wooden door by Morris J. Sheppard.

A paneled door adds ornamentation while enhancing security with its solid wood face.

Craftsman Morris J. Sheppard modeled this stair on the one in the famous 1908 Green & Greene Gamble house in Pasadena. Each board has been carefully rounded and sanded to a smooth finish. The pins and pegs accentuate in a celebration of the carpenter's art.

A carved cap on a newel post reflects themes from nature.

A tri-paneled stained glass mural overlooks the landing halfway up this stairwell of turned balustrades and carved newel posts. Quarter-sawn boards create a zigzag of tiger stripes on the kickboards to delight those who undertake the climb.

The end post of this stairwell flares in keeping with classic bungalow-style. Swiss variations were popular, as seen in the calmes of the upper windowpanes and in the heraldic symbols cut out in the staircase balusters.

Stairs finish with a rounded flourish at the base of a U-shaped stairwell.

Wood paneling fills floor to ceiling in this wonderful stairwell.

Dark finishes still allow the wood grain to show in this central stairwell typical of arts and crafts construction.

Paneling wraps a staircase modeled on arts and crafts style.

# Woodwork & Built-ins

A window nook is covered in wonderful cherry, mahogany paneling, and lavish decorative detail.

**OPPOSITE:**
A window seat was created in a bay window, preserving storage space with a small, trap door. A triangular pattern in the window mullions evokes Swiss styling, which was also popular during the Arts and Crafts era.

Simple casement windows crown a built-in window seat.

A matching pair of built-in bookcases frames a doorway outlined in solid wood.

Pocket doors are a wonderful space saver, preserving room that can be furnished without having to accommodate doors that swing.

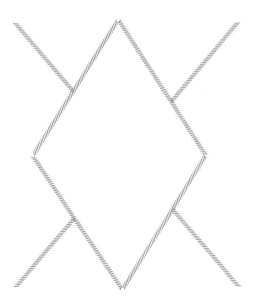

Diamond panes are repeated in both lead and wood in this Swiss style craftsman home.
Above, paneled beams create a classic ceiling relief.

RIGHT:
Close-ups reveal the molding profiles of
crown molding and door frames.

139

Crown molding built up in many layers creates an impressive finale to a room furnished with antiques.

Molding creates a shelf atop a doorway, built up with layers of wood.

Woodwork outweighs glass in a window frame, highlighting the carpenter's enthusiasm.

Layers of molding ascend to paneled beams.

Paneled columns, flaring at the base, are an expected accouterment in the open passageways between bungalow rooms.

Woodwork forms a carved cap for a paneled column.

Corbels adorn a plate shelf, overshadowed by a beautiful, coffered ceiling.

Egg and dart molding caps a column.

Extreme attention was paid to the molding of coffered ceiling and paneled walls.

Gingko leaves fall around a doorbell plate.

A mail slot has been painted so many times, the metal is indistinguishable from the wood shingles.

Hand-forged brass door handle

Bells descend, reminding admirers to announce their presence.

A solid door pull, lock, and knocker present a formidable welcome.

Antique knocker

Asian influence is evidenced in a dragon's head knocker surrounded by clouds.

147

A *fleur-de-lis* caps fancy hardware.

A door brace bears the marks of its hand-wrought nature.

Antique door latches and locks

148

An elegant doorknob and pull, with straight Wright-like lines.

Antique brass doorknobs

Historically, it seems, knockers were designed to intimidate would-be callers.

Pulls and handles help date built-in cabinetry.

A vintage door pull and doorbell worthy of the rich oak surround.

A mailbox celebrates craftsmanship and evokes an era when junk mail was less bulky.

A brass lock, with a lion's head to ward off danger.

Antique ironwork adorns a fireplace, overlooked by wise old owls and framed in earthen tile.

RIGHT:
An antique mail grate

A metal grate beautifies an access panel.

A heating grate is an easily overlooked antique treasure.

Artist Heather McLarty was inspired by earlier craftsmen when she wrought this *faux bois* gate, adorned with plump billiard fruits.

# Glass

Beveled glass magnifies a leaded frame.

A leaded glass door and built-in cabinet complement each other with craftsmanship that celebrates the wood's open grains.

Fish swim in a glass pond, blue lotus blooming above.

Here beveled glass adds delight and distortion to a front door window.

Stained glass evokes the popular theme of abstract flora.

In a nod to getting back to nature, a robed figure sits amidst a pastoral scene playing music.

# LIGHTING

**TOP ROW:**
A pendant lamp is an example of exquisite glasswork.

An exquisitely wrought chandelier cradles handmade glass.

What do you do when you've won so many Tonys and Oscars you can hardly count them? Songwriter and music producer Jerry Leiber's solution was to turn this one into a lamp, with a tasteful, Arts and Crafts era inspired shade for Oscars' upper torso. One of his Grammy Awards sits nearby on the mantel, just to the left of his Songwriter's Hall of Fame award.

**BOTTOM ROW:**
Glass hangs like a drape on this exquisite arts and crafts antique that has been re-wired.

Steel lacework takes center stage on this incredible piece of craftsmanship.

An incandescent bulb is in keeping with the original fixture set in a beautifully coffered ceiling.

An incandescent bulb burns in a ceiling fixture.

A beautiful wood sconce imitates its metal cousins and matches the warm tones of a hallway's rich wood paneling.

Overhead fluorescents are given a period-worthy disguise with wood framing and golden glass.

Looking straight up at the ceiling, a trio of stained glass panels are beautifully framed and backlit to illuminate the room below.

Modern incandescent bulbs still complement the glory of this ironwork chandelier.

Hand-cast glass accompanies wrought iron in an elaborate, symmetrical sconce.

In classic arts and crafts style, a wall lamp created for the American market imitates Japanese style.

A wonderful pendant lamp is suspended from beaded iron chains.

Four frosty pendant bulbs hang from a simple antique chandelier.

Bent glass creates a multi-hued diffuser for an antique sconce.

Modern LED lighting illuminates a stained glass window in the adjacent room from behind. The tiny components are cleverly concealed by panels adorned with wallpaper of the period.

An extended chandelier is in keeping with a paneled stairwell terminating in an imported tiger panel.

An antique table lamp illuminates a collection of antique photographs and stereoscope cards.

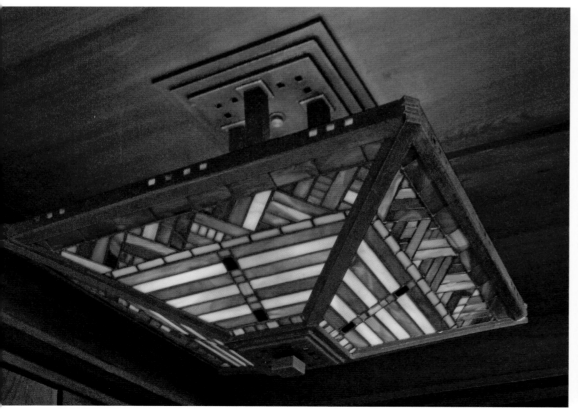

Stained glass softens the light from a ceiling fixture.

Stained glass work is arranged in an intricate pattern from the Wright school of straight lines.

Wood frames a leaded glass fixture with abstract shapes in colorful glass.

Colorful glass adorns a classic arts and crafts wall fixture.

Thick, hand-formed glass lends organic texture to lighting.

An antique lantern with leaded glass

Spanish influence is evidenced in an antique glass and iron lantern.

Japanese lanterns had a profound effect on arts and crafts artists and decorators and were widely reproduced. The smaller lantern on the brick wall is a contemporary lantern in arts and crafts style, notice the solar panels on this sustainable addition to the landscaping.

Frosted globes and a matching wall sconce represent the more commercial options available in the early days of electrical lighting.

Asian influence was an important element in arts and crafts design.

Golden hues swirl in the stained glass slabs of this substantial pendant lamp.

A bronze beauty plays with the beaded shade of an antique lamp.

An antique wall sconce fashioned with a Japanese aesthetic.

Yellow glass casts a welcoming glow.

Stained glass, wrought iron, and careful craftsmanship elevate an outdoor lighting fixture.

## ACCESSORIES

In conclusion, we share some of the best gems—vignettes of antique treasures from the era this book celebrates.

Music is celebrated in relief next to a delightfully crafted clay pitcher.

**BOTTOM ROW:**
A marriage of basketry and ironwork, a woodworker's frame, and an artist celebrating the simplistic, this collection of antiques embodies the arts and crafts spirit.

A stein evokes the Egyptian falcon and a fluted goblet seems suitable for a queen of the Nile. Egyptian art has informed craftsman and creative people working in various styles throughout history, including the Arts and Crafts era.

The earthen qualities of clay and the hand of the potter were highly celebrated elements of arts and crafts.

Posters and ephemera celebrate early tourism in California. Collector Chuck Mauch is pressed for space for his incredible collection of antiques, and has resorted to displaying art overhead. His desk is furnished with exquisite antiques from his favorite era.

A collection of period antiques— handmade tile, lighting, and a glass vase.

An assembly of antique vessels adorns a small bookshelf.

Embroidery and fiber arts are less likely to stand the test of time, making these antiques that much more precious.

A collection of precious art pottery on display.

A bevel-edged mirror celebrates nonconformity over antique serving ware and a classic lamp.